PHARAOH'S BUTLER & BAKER
THE UNKNOWN POWER OF FORGIVENESS

BY C.C. SKYE

WestBow Press books may be ordered through booksellers or by contacting:

WestBow Press
A Division of Thomas Nelson & Zondervan
1663 Liberty Drive
Bloomington, IN 47403
www.westbowpress.com
844-714-3454

Interior Image Credit: Hajra Mazhar

ISBN: 978-1-6642-9693-0 (sc)
ISBN: 978-1-6642-9694-7 (e)

Library of Congress Control Number: 2023906283

Print information available on the last page.

WestBow Press rev. date: 4/18/2023

WESTBOW
PRESS®
A DIVISION OF THOMAS NELSON
& ZONDERVAN

I would like to dedicate this book to:

God

God your servant has now completed this mission given by You. I thank You for guiding and providing everything I've needed to get this done. All the glory and all the honor belongs to You.

My Grandchildren

Dear Kamari, Damia, Raven and RJ, this is my inheritance to you. Never forget that you are loved and valued and to follow your God given dreams. How do you do this? By remembering and acting upon the values taught within these pages. May God richly bless and keep you.

Love Grandma

In Egypt, a long time ago,
there lived a butler and baker who worked for Pharaoh.

They lived in Egypt with buildings called pyramids which still, today, we know not how they did.

Butler was in charge of Pharaoh's house
of everyone there, even the mouse.

Baker was in charge of all Pharaoh's food.
His tasty treats put him in a happy mood.

4

Pharaoh was their godlike king,
which means he could do almost anything.

One terrible day, Pharaoh yelled,
"Take both Butler and Baker to jail!"

Did Butler steal Pharaoh's ring
and think he was king?

Did Baker eat Pharaoh's pie
and then tell a lie?

We don't know this part because

ONLY GOD KNOWS THE HEART

Would they depend on Jesus and confess their sins
or trust in themselves, thinking they could win?

10

Then one day, both Butler
and Baker dreamed
and pondered what it could mean.

Not knowing the answer, they became sad.
In their hearts, both knew this could be bad.

A man named Joseph was also there.
All prisoners were under his care.
He'd been taken prisoner too.
But for something he didn't do.

13

Joseph then said, "Do not these answers to God belong? Tell me your dreams because He's never wrong."

15

Butler told about three branches on a vine, that was squeezed into wine.
It was given to Pharaoh in a cup, for him to drink up.

Joseph listened carefully
to Butler's tail
and said, "In three days,
you'll be released from jail."

Pharaoh will put you back
in charge of his house
over all the people,
even the mouse.

Joseph told Butler, "Don't forget about me. Please tell Pharaoh to set me free."

What happened next filled Baker's heart with dread
because Joseph told him in three days, he'd be dead.

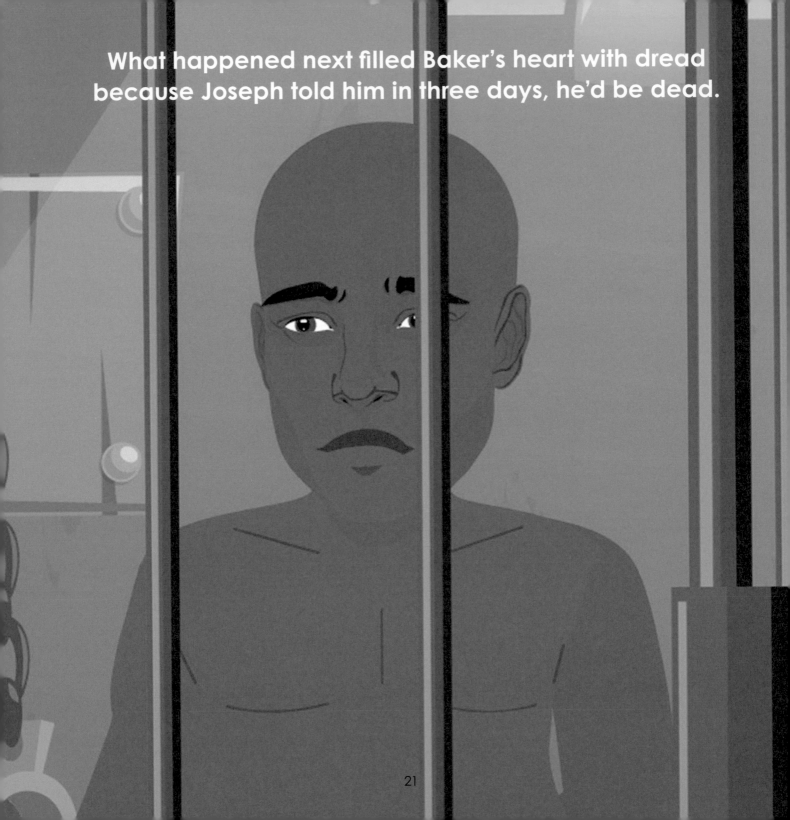

Butler's sentence was different because he'd confessed before asking for forgiveness, so did his part. Jesus was then able to come into his heart.

22

Baker had decided to go a different way.
Thinking, "I can do this and not have to pay."

Jesus promised Butler other gifts too.
Then whispered in his sleeping
ear, "I will free you."

Butler was pardoned and then set free.
If God we trust, He'll do the same for you and me.

25

Only through Jesus there's a way out.
So don't be like Baker and foolishly doubt.

When facing trials, be like Butler and rest your case,
not on yourself, but on God's amazing grace.

Thank You For Reading My Book!

I really appreciate all of your feedback
and I love hearing what you have to say.

I need your input to make my future books better.

Please take two minutes now to leave a
helpful review on Amazon letting me know
what you thought of the book.

Thanks so much and God Bless!!!

C.C. Skye

Printed in the United States
by Baker & Taylor Publisher Services